If not wanting to break the silence is perhaps the ethos of haiku, and the gentler side of tanka, then plum blossom should be the colour of a cellphone junkyard. Galaxies turn within a river's darkness as I step into an owl's dream. Salzer's work is a dreamlike magic, holding back the chaos.

Alan Summers
Founder, *Call of the Page*

Whether Jacob Salzer is writing about cellphone junkyards, an owl's dream, or koto strings, *Unplugged—* is a study in awareness and simplicity. Skipping stones with his father or recognizing his mother's stories in his veins, Salzer pays tribute to his family and to the world that surrounds him. A beautiful collection.

Terry Ann Carter
Author of *Tokaido* (Red Moon Press, 2017) A Distinguished Book Award winner

Unplugged—, a micropoetry collection by Jacob Salzer, connects us with the intricacies of nature that we usually overlook or miss due to the fast-paced life. The brevity, freshness, and vividness of the poems reflect how remarkably the poet has interwoven his thoughts and feelings with some deep personal experiences. I highly recommend this book.

Hifsa Ashraf
Award-Winning poet, co-commentator at the *Haiku Commentary* blog and author of *wildflowers: haiku & tanka*, *her deep-rooted scars: haiku, monostiches & cherita, Her Fading Henna Tattoo: A collection of haiku poems based on domestic violence against women (received honourable mentions in the Touchstone distinguished book awards and HSA merit book awards)*, *Running After Shadows: A Collection of Haiku Destigmatizing Mental Illness in Women*, and *Working with Demons*

Unplugged— is a delicious encounter with the mysteries and relationships of the animate world. In each haiku and tanka, Jacob has provided an unassuming space for the reader to feel and hear the wordless language of trees, water, fire, and air. Captured in moments of wonder, awe, and respect for our Great Mother, Jacob's words resonate and spread out like branches, inviting us to gently pause, rest, and join with Nature in honest communion. Jacob's poetry is a healing medicine in a world that is so fast-paced, we often miss the opportunity to slow down and engage with life in pure and simple ways.

Unplugged— encourages us to be awake and aware of our humanness and oneness with the Earth as we become part of something much larger than ourselves.

Michelle Hyatt
Co-author of *Echoes: A Collection of Linked-Verse Poetry*

Salzer's haiku and tanka in this collection display a clear connection between the human experience and nature, with emotive and poignant tones flowing throughout. This clarity comes even when he reaches more into imaginative and experimental expression. Like great haiku poets before him, Salzer writes from a genuine place that opens the heart of readers—revealing the compassion we have hidden behind our many facades.

Nicholas Klacsanzky
Founder and co-editor of the *Haiku Commentary* blog; co-author of *Zen and Son: Haiku from Two Generations,* and *How Many Become One: A Haiku Sequence*

Jacob D. Salzer's *Unplugged—* is a refreshing release from the busyness of today's fast-paced tech world. It invites us to pause, meander into, and experience the richness of life present in mundane yet profound ways.

His words immediately connect us with nature where we can enter into "the oak tree" where "lifetimes echo" or enjoy the "wake of a seal" in a summer sunset on Olympia's bay. Evocative, sensitive, and compassionate, these poems of haiku and tanka bring us in contact with our own deep, kind, and intuitive nature that Jacob reveals in this book.

Diana Saltoon
Author of *Wife, Just Let Go: Zen, Alzheimer's, and Love*, with Robert Briggs (2017), *Tea and Ceremony* (2004), *The Common Book of Consciousness* (1990), and *Four Hands: Green Gulch Poems* (1987)

Unplugged—

Haiku & Tanka

Jacob D. Salzer

Also by Jacob D. Salzer

BOOKS
The Sound of Rain (Haiku)
Birds With No Names (Haiku)
Fog Between Mountains (Haiku)
A Steady Beam of Light (Haiku)
Mare Liberum (Haiku & Tanka)
Origins (Haibun)
The Last Days of Winter (Poetry)

ANTHOLOGIES & COLLABORATIONS
Yanty's Butterfly
New Bridges
Half A Rainbow
Desert Rain
How Many Become One (with Nicholas Klacsanzky) (Haiku Sequence)
Echoes: A Collection of Linked-Verse Poetry (with Michelle Hyatt)

This book is dedicated to:

Mother Earth

My friend Michelle Hyatt for her
kindness and friendship

My family, for all the good times,
camping trips and visits to the beach

My haiku friends (all of them)

Our ancestors

Unplugged—

Haiku & Tanka

ISBN: 978-1-387-93717-2

Unplugged— Haiku & Tanka

acknowledgments

I would like to thank the editors of the
following journals and websites:

Chrysanthemum
First Frost
Frogpond
Haiku Commentary
Hedgerow
Heliosparrow
Is/Let
Kingfisher
Presence
Ribbons
The Haiku Foundation
The Heron's Nest
The Living Haiku Anthology

I would like to thank haiku poets in
Haiku Nook G+ and the Portland Haiku
Group for their contributions. I would
like to thank Alan Summers for his
encouragement and support.

I would like to acknowledge the Haiku Society of America for their work with the international haiku community.

I would like to thank Michael Dylan Welch, Nicholas Klacsanzky, and everyone in the Seabeck haiku community.

I'd like to thank the HSA president Jay Friedenberg for inviting me to serve as an HSA mentor in their mentorship program.

I'd also like to thank my mentees: Mary McCormack, j rap, Lisa Gerlits and Ian Gwin for their kindness and participation.

I would like to thank Don Baird and the Living Haiku Anthology staff for publishing a page of my haiku.

Lastly, I thank my family, for everything they've done and continue to bring to life.

contents

"Follow Nature and return to Nature."

Matsuo Bashō

"Every day is a journey, and the journey itself is home."

Matsuo Bashō

lost
in my digital footprint . . .
the weight of snow

unheard rainstorm
drowning within
a digital sea

the only color
in a cellphone junkyard . . .
plum blossom

unplugged—
I walk into the forest
without a sound

Unplugged—

picking kale—
the darkened veins
in grandma's hands

smell of moss
on our ancestor's headstone
my father's shadow

forest mist . . .
thoughts drift
into other worlds

plum blossom . . .
before the baby
has a name

not wanting
to break our silence
evening fog . . .
through cracks in ice
the buds of yellow roses

scent of green tea
in my travel mug
the forest's darkness

autumn evening . . .
I step into
the owl's dream

grandpa's stream
the long journey
of mountain rain

grandma's ashes . . .
the Columbia River flows
into the sea

heavy net
the eyes of a fish
become still

in the wet garden strands of her leaving

an acquaintance . . .
the bridge disappears
in evening mist

dream tunnel a worm enters the fallen apple

piercing
Horseshoe Falls
the house sparrow's song

For Michelle

hidden faces
in the Makah totem pole
drifting fog . . .
in the palms of my hands
the smell of salmon

darkness in the old Redwood voices

sleeping samurai . . .
the ladybug sways
on a blade of grass

holding our breath . . .
the Orca whale
rocks the boat

family game night
the lantern's hum
gathering moths

summer sunset
on Olympia's bay
the wake of a seal

distant thunder ...
lifetimes echo
in the oak tree

winter wind
between passing clouds
the warmth of stars
I imagine
you are still here

past lives
from my acoustic guitar
the scent of spruce

at the edge
of a forest map
winter rain . . .
galaxies turn
in the river's darkness

gray whale teeth
around the Shaman's neck
songs at sea

tea conversation —
a word slips
into koto strings

mother's tone —
a blue bird sings
in crystal cold rain

sand castle . . .
a thought crumbles
in the child's laughter

call of geese
on the Columbia River
the ebb and flow
of stars

a long pause
in the conversation
about grandma's death
the sound of wind
between mountains

her whispers in the dark rain falling asleep

moonlight
in the overgrown cemetery
frozen shadows
how many thoughts
have I buried?

a homeless man
mumbles something to himself
winter wind

cold wind seeking a flame— the river's darkness

charcoal
in a hollow tree
the scent of apples

first impression . . .
my footprints
lost in snow

sign language
the stories of a farm
in her hands

wichoni mini
in the darkening woods
my footsteps

---

wichoni mini = life-giving rains (see notes)

quiet stream . . .
the maple leaf drifts
into a galaxy

soft wind
beneath the tree
a child's grave

lifetimes
in the veins of my hands
mother's stories
moonlight gently reveals
a leaf's skeleton

invasive species
lingering in my hands
the scent of ivy

skipping stones
with father
ripples collide

how many
become one
sound of rain

the last bend in a river the endless sea

sea shell —
the old man curls
into a fetus

notes

"gray whale teeth" haiku on page 25:

"The relationship between [the] Makah [tribe] and whales is very old. Ozette deposits dating from 2,000 years ago hold humpback and gray whale bones and barbs from harpoons."

"The next step was to tow the whale home. Hopefully, the distance would only be a few miles if its spirit had heeded prayers to swim for the beach…Songs eased the paddling and welcomed the whale to the village. The songs welcomed the returning hunters and praised the power that made it all possible."

Source: https://makah.com/makah-tribal-info/whaling/

"*wichoni mini*" haiku on page 38:

wichoni mini is a Sioux Native American term that means life-giving rains.

Source: Mother Earth Spirituality by Ed McGaa (HarperCollins, 1990)

publication credits

6   *The Heron's Nest, Volume XXIII, Number 4: December, 2021; Desert Rain: Haiku Nook: An Anthology (Lulu, 2022); Haiku Commentary Blog*

7   *Paper Mountains: 2020 Seabeck Haiku Getaway Anthology (Haiku Northwest Press, 2021)*

8   *First Frost, issue #3, 2022; Desert Rain: Haiku Nook: An Anthology (Lulu, 2022)*

9   *2021 Seabeck Haiku Anthology (Haiku Northwest Press, 2022)*

10 *Featured in the Bristol Museum & Art Gallery Masters of Japanese Prints, 2020 website exhibition — Inspired and displayed with a print: Fishing Boats with Nets under Ryōgoku Bridge, 1790 by Kitagawa Utamaro I (1753-1806) Mb4757:*

https://exhibitions.bristolmuseums.org.uk/japanese-prints/haikus/

11 *Is/Let, 2021*

12 *A Quiet Stream: A Haiku Blog*

13 *Heliosparrow Poetry Journal, April 24, 2021*

30   *Hedgerow #137, 2022*

31   *Hedgerow #138, 2022*

32   *Ribbons, Fall Issue 2022; also recorded on
     The Magical Mystery Tour WGDR radio
     show:*

*https://soundcloud.com/wgdr/the-magical-
mystery-tour-mar-4-2022-haiku-linked-verse-
poetry-w-michelle-hyatt-jacob-salzer*

33   *Hedgerow #137, 2022*

34   *Is/Let, 2021*

35   *A Quiet Stream: A Haiku Blog*

36   *A Quiet Stream: A Haiku Blog*

37   *Presence #70, 2021*

38   *A Quiet Stream: A Haiku Blog*

39   *A Quiet Stream: A Haiku Blog*

40   *A Quiet Stream: A Haiku Blog*

41   *A Quiet Stream: A Haiku Blog*

42   *A Quiet Stream: A Haiku Blog*

bio

Jacob D. Salzer grew up in the Pacific Northwest. He has been writing haiku and related forms since 2006 when he took a haiku class at The Evergreen State College: *The Way of Haiku and Haibun* taught by Kate Crow. Since that time, Jacob has published his haiku, tanka, and haibun in numerous journals. He is the author of *Mare Liberum: Haiku & Tanka* (Lulu, 2020) and the co-author of *Echoes: A Collection of Linked-Verse Poetry* (Lulu, 2020) with Michelle Hyatt.

Jacob is the founder & editor of the *Haiku Poet Interviews Blog,* dedicated to interviewing haiku poets internationally: https://haikupoetinterviews.wordpress.com. Jacob has served as an HSA (Haiku Society of America) haiku mentor since 2021. He also serves as commentator for the *Haiku Commentary* blog along with the editors Nicholas Klacsanzky and Hifsa Ashraf: https://haikucommentary.wordpress.com/.

He served as the managing editor of two Haiku Nook anthologies: *Yanty's Butterfly* (dedicated to haiku poet Yanty Tjiam) and *Half A Rainbow* (dedicated to haiku poet Rachel Sutcliffe). Jacob is also an active member of the Portland Haiku Group, where he served as the managing editor of the Portland Haiku Group anthology, *New Bridges*, dedicated to haiku poet Johnny Baranski. He recently edited *Desert Rain: Haiku Nook: An Anthology* (Lulu, 2022) dedicated to Martha Magenta and the 600+ million people who don't have access to clean water.

Jacob enjoys spending time with his friends and family and has several interests, including: painting, drawing, photography, music, poetry, meditation, indigenous culture, exercise, nutrition, neurobiology, medical coding, reading, editing, professional networking, and social activism. As a musician, he enjoys playing piano, guitar and tabla drums from India. He frequently utilizes *Americans of Conscience* to advocate for a better U.S. and world: https://americansofconscience.com/.

Inspired by the Great Seal of the United States, *E Pluribus Unum*, a Latin phrase that translates to: Out of Many, One, Jacob values respect and diversity, and is dedicated to creating new bridges and community in a world that far too often appears violent and fragmented.

Jacob frequently writes about water and his favorite color is blue. *Unplugged—* is his second collection of haiku and tanka inspired by Mother Earth and his friend Michelle Hyatt.

To read more of Jacob's poetry, please visit:

https://jsalzer.wixsite.com/mareliberumhaiku

Additional Websites

Haiku Poet Interviews
haikupoetinterviews.wordpress.com/

Haiku Commentary
https://haikucommentary.wordpress.com/

The Haiku Society of America
http://www.hsa-haiku.org/

Echoes: A Collection of Linked-Verse
jsalzer.wixsite.com/echoes

Yanty's Butterfly
jsalzer.wixsite.com/yantysbutterfly

Half A Rainbow
jsalzer.wixsite.com/halfarainbowhaiku

New Bridges
jsalzer.wixsite.com/portlandhaikugroup

Desert Rain
https://jsalzer.wixsite.com/desertrain

"The river goes on roaring, without knowing if it's day or night, it goes on without distraction, and does not know of past or future or any measurement of time.

The waves appear separate, but they are forever one with the vast ocean and its unfathomable depths. Just as each snowflake is different yet made of the same substance, we are unique expressions of one life. May we recognize this so we can stop the violence, celebrate our differences and dance in unison, in synchronicity.

My life is not my life, as the river of this life is only a silent song that will soon fade away into the wordless depths of a nameless sea."

Jacob D. Salzer